BEARED DRAGON

Complete Guide on How to Train
and Keep a Bearded Dragon
(Including How to Know the Age
of Your Bearded Dragon)

FRANCESCO MARCO

Copyright©2018

TABLE OF CONTENTS

CHAPTER 1 3

INTRODUCTION 3

CHAPTER 2 5

HOW TO SETUP FOR YOUR BEARDED DRAGON 5

CHAPTER 3 13

HOW TO FEED YOUR PET 13

CHAPTER 4 20

HOW TO PICK UP YOUR BEARDED DRAGON20

CHAPTER 5 25

HOW TO CLEAN YOUR BEARDED DRAGON..25

THE END 28

CHAPTER 1

INTRODUCTION

Native to Australia, bearded dragons were first introduced to the United States in the mid-1990s, and their popularity as pets has increased dramatically in the past two decades. Largely considered the most docile creatures among the lizard world, beardies (as they're affectionately known to those who love them) are a lot like dogs, but with scales. As natural desert dwellers, bearded dragons require a specific environment and special care to thrive in other climates. Here's what you need to know to keep your new beardie happy and healthy.

CHAPTER 2

HOW TO SETUP FOR YOUR BEARDED DRAGON

1. Decide on a habitat. Bearded dragons are commonly kept in glass tanks, while some owners set their pets up in a cage made from melamine, PVC, or ABS plastic. If you're the DIY type you can make your own habitat, or you might find it simpler to buy a **starter kit**that comes with other basics. Another option is a vision tank, which is professionally made using a single, molded piece of plastic (although they're pricey).

2. Choose the right size tank or cage. Baby beardies need a habitat at least 20 gallons in size. As your bearded dragon grows, however, you'll need to upgrade his space based on his size:

- 10- to 16-inch dragons: 40+ gallons
- 16- to 20-inch dragons: 50-75 gallons
- 20+ inch dragons: 75-120 gallons (larger is better)

Purchasing a habitat big enough to accommodate an adult gives your beardie ample room to grow, plus you won't need to spend money upgrading your tank later.

2. Equip the habitat with full-spectrum lighting. Beardies are native to the desert regions in Australia, so they require full-spectrum light (not your standard household light bulb) for 12 to 14 hours per day. There are several options, such as **this Zoo Med bulb** or **this bulb from Evergreen Pet Supplies**.

**3. Get a basking bulb and a
perch.** Your beardie also needs
a **basking bulb**, as well as a way
to get close to the heat emitted
from it (they're usually placed on
top of the tank), such as a **reptile
hammock** or a **basking ramp**.

**4. Get the right housing for
your lights.** Look for the right
housing for these bulbs;
a **terrarium hood** sized
appropriately for the habitat and
the bulb size works well for full-
spectrum bulbs, while basking
bulbs usually fit **dome fixtures**.

5. Get a thermometer that measures temperature and humidity. Temperature gauges like **this one** are designed for reptile tanks. One side of the tank (the basking side) should be warmer (90-93 degrees Fahrenheit for adults) and the other side cooler (80-90 degrees Fahrenheit). Baby beardies and juveniles require slightly different temperatures. At night, turn the lights off and allow the temperature to drop to 70 to 75 degrees Fahrenheit. Get two thermometers to monitor temperatures on both sides of the tank.

6. Add substrate. Loose-particle substrate like sand may seem logical, but it's not a good choice for bearded dragons as it can lead to blockages and other health concerns. You can simply use shredded newspaper as substrate, or get a specially designed **reptile carpet**.

7. Add some decor. There are a few other accessories that will make your beardie's habitat feel more like home:

- **Tank backgrounds.** Desert backgrounds like <u>this</u> look similar to a beardie's natural environment.

- **Rock dens or "hides." <u>These enclosures</u>** give your beardie some shade when he needs to get out of the direct light and a spot to hide when he needs some alone time. They can also double as a basking perch when strategically placed.

- **Shallow food and water bowls.** Water bowls that are

too deep can increase the humidity level in the habitat, so a shallow bowl like **this one** is best. The same style dish can be used for food.

CHAPTER 3
HOW TO FEED YOUR PET

1. Provide access to water. If you live in a dry climate, you can leave a shallow bowl of fresh, clean water in the tank all the time. If you live in a moist climate, give your beardie access to a water dish for a few hours each day or every other day.

2. Keep a spray bottle on hand. If your beardie doesn't regularly drink from his water dish, gently mist him with water using a spray bottle. Most beardies will lick drops of water from their nose, just like their wild cousins do in the rain. Continue misting your beardie until he stops drinking.

3. Bearded dragons need a varied diet. They require a mix of insects and worms such as:

- Crickets
- Phoenix worms
- Horn worms
- Butterworms
- Super worms

Greens and vegetables are essential, too. Staples include:

- Collard greens
- Turnip greens
- Mustard greens
- Butternut squash
- Okra
- Yellow squash
- Sweet potato
- Mango
- Papaya

Other greens and vegetables can be fed occasionally, and other foods should be avoided completely, such as:

- Lettuce
- Spinach
- Avocado
- Wild-caught insects
- Citrus fruits
- Rhubarb

Get a complete list of safe vegetables **here** (**plants** and **frui ts**, too), and a full list of unsafe or poisonous foods **here**.

An adult bearded dragon's diet should consist of about 25 to 30% insects and other prey and 70 to 75% plant matter. Chop all fruits and vegetables finely. Feeder insects should be no larger than

the space between your beardie's
eyes; most pet stores offer feeder
insects in various sizes.

**4. Provide
supplements. <u>Multivitamins</u>** e
nsure beardie is getting all the
essential nutrients he needs. They
need additional Vitamin D3
supplements and calcium, both of
which come in a **<u>powder
supplement</u>**.

**5. Dust insects and sprinkle
salads with calcium
powder.** Coat insects in calcium
powder immediately before each
feeding. Simply place some

powder in an enclosed container, add crickets, and shake it up. Sprinkle salads with the same powder.

5. Gut-load all insects prior to feeding your beardie. This is easily done by layering some fish food or **cricket feed** in the bottom of your **cricket-keeper**. Add some small chunks of raw vegetables (carrots, sweet potatoes, or orange slices) or use **water pillows**. Let feeder insects feast for 24-48 hours prior to your beardie's meal.

6. Use commercial bearded dragon food as a supplement. Commercial **bearded dragon food** is best used as a treat or supplement rather than a main dietary source. Use it to give a little variety to your beardie's salad greens.

CHAPTER 4

HOW TO PICK UP YOUR BEARDED DRAGON

1. Wash your hands before touching your beardie. Your beardie can pick up germs and illnesses from your hands if they aren't clean.

2. Approach slowly. No one likes to be ambushed, beardies included. Be calm and confident. Do not interrupt your bearded dragon in the middle of a meal or a nap.

3. Don't reach from above. And don't wiggle your finger at him. He'll probably think it's a worm, and that ends well for no one. If you back him into a corner, he'll probably feel threatened, with a similar outcome as the finger-wiggling exercise.

5. Gently pet your beardie. Gently touch him so he gets used to the feeling of your hand.

6. Read your bearded dragon's cues. If he closes his eyes or blinks, he's comfortable enough for you to pick him up. A black beard means he's stressed out or mad – a clear signal that it's time for you to back down for now.

7. Scoop him up with the palm of your hand. Slide your hand under his belly and gently lift him while supporting his body with your hand. Always support all of his legs. After removing him from his habitat, let him rest on your arm, chest, or leg – wherever you (and your beardie) are most comfortable. Pet him along (not against) the direction of his scales.

8. If your dragon's belly starts to feel cool, it's time to return him to his habitat. During the cooler months, you may need to limit your beardie's adventures to several shorter sessions each day.

9. Have fun with your beardie. Some people get <u>reptile harnesses</u> to take their pets on outdoor adventures when it's warm enough. Get a <u>reptile carrier</u> for vet trips or car rides. Or, let him go for a swim in a plastic container filled with

shallow water (but treat it
with **water conditioner** first).

**10. Return him to his
habitat.** Support his body in the
same way you did when picking
him up to place him back into his
habitat.

**11. Wash your hands
(again).** Wash your hands after
handling your beardie with anti-
bacterial soap to avoid salmonella
and other nasty germs and
bacteria.

CHAPTER 5

HOW TO CLEAN YOUR BEARDED DRAGON

1. Choose a container. Use a plastic storage tote like <u>this</u>, a children's swimming pool or <u>**mini-tub**</u>, the bathtub, or anything in between. Make sure the sides are high enough that your beardie can't easily escape.

2. Fill with shallow water. The water should be no higher than the joints where your dragon's legs meet his body.

3. Make sure the water is the appropriate temperature. The ideal temperature is between 85 and 100 degrees Fahrenheit. Your beardie can soak for 10 to 30 minutes. If the water gets too cool, add some warm water and remove some cool water, keeping the water at the right level.

4. Condition the water. Water conditioners for reptiles are readily available in pet stores and online. **Zoo Med's Repti Safe** is a popular option, and it takes only

a few drops of water to make
ordinary tap water safe.

5. Don't use soap. Most bearded
dragons will drink water when
going for a swim. Plus, cleaning
agents can be damaging to their
skin.

**6. Use a cup to pour water
over your beardie's back.** You
don't need to scrub your bearded
dragon. Gently pour cups of bath
water down his back and tail.

7. Remove old skin. If your
beardie has shedding skin, you can
help him shed by wiping those

areas gently with a washcloth or soft-bristled toothbrush. Don't do this if your beardie is still actively shedding or if the skin does not come off easily without resistance.

8. Dry him off and warm him up. When bath time is over, place him on a soft towel and gently pat him dry. Put him back in his habitat so he can bask and warm up.

THE END